HOW TO DRAW FANTASY ART

DRAGONS

Jim Hansen and John Burns

FOR SALE
WITHDRAWN
FROM STOCK

BOROUGH OF POOLE	
550457827 0	
J743	£6.99
2007	PETERS

D0486723

First published in 2007 by Franklin Watts

Copyright © 2007 Arcturus Publishing Limited

Franklin Watts
338 Euston Road
London NW1 3BH

Franklin Watts Australia
Level 17/207 Kent St, Sydney, NSW 2000

Produced by Arcturus Publishing Limited,
26/27 Bickels Yard, 151–153 Bermondsey Street, London SE1 3HA

The right of Jim Hansen to be identified as the author of this work has been asserted by
him in accordance with the Copyright, Designs and Patents Act 1988.

Artwork and text: Jim Hansen
Colourist: John Burns
Editor: Alex Woolf
Designer: Jane Hawkins

A CIP catalogue record for this book is available from the British Library.

Dewey Decimal Classification Number: 743'.87

ISBN: 978 0 7496 7651 3

Printed in China

Franklin Watts is a division of Hachette Children's Books.

Contents

Introduction

Of all the creatures of fantasy and folklore, there is nothing that quite grabs the imagination like the dragon. These fire-breathing monsters appear in the myths and stories of cultures all over the world. Sometimes they are kind and helpful. At other times they are the very essence of evil.

Eastern dragons are mainly of the kind and helpful variety. The Chinese dragon is perhaps the most good-natured of all, and is a symbol of good luck. Spring in China is the season for 'dragon processions', held to welcome their return from a winter spent underground.

In the West, dragons are seen as the ultimate nightmare. They represent all that is wicked and evil in the world – though our fear of them is mixed with awe. With their fiery breath, sharp teeth, and powerful wings, these magnificent creatures have always demanded our respect.

So, whether you prefer the beautiful, snake-like Eastern dragons, or the fearsome, deadly Western dragons – have fun drawing the beasts in this book.

EQUIPMENT

The success of your work is largely down to the quality of your tools, so to get the best out of your drawing, you'll need to gather together the items listed below.

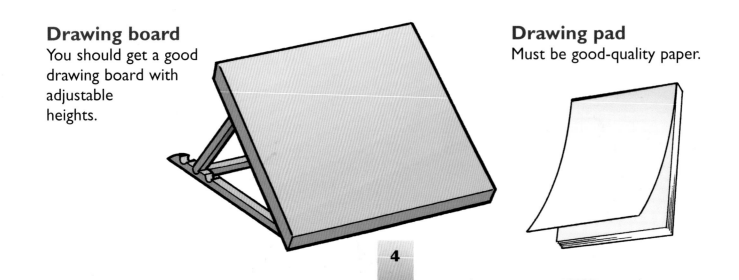

Drawing board
You should get a good drawing board with adjustable heights.

Drawing pad
Must be good-quality paper.

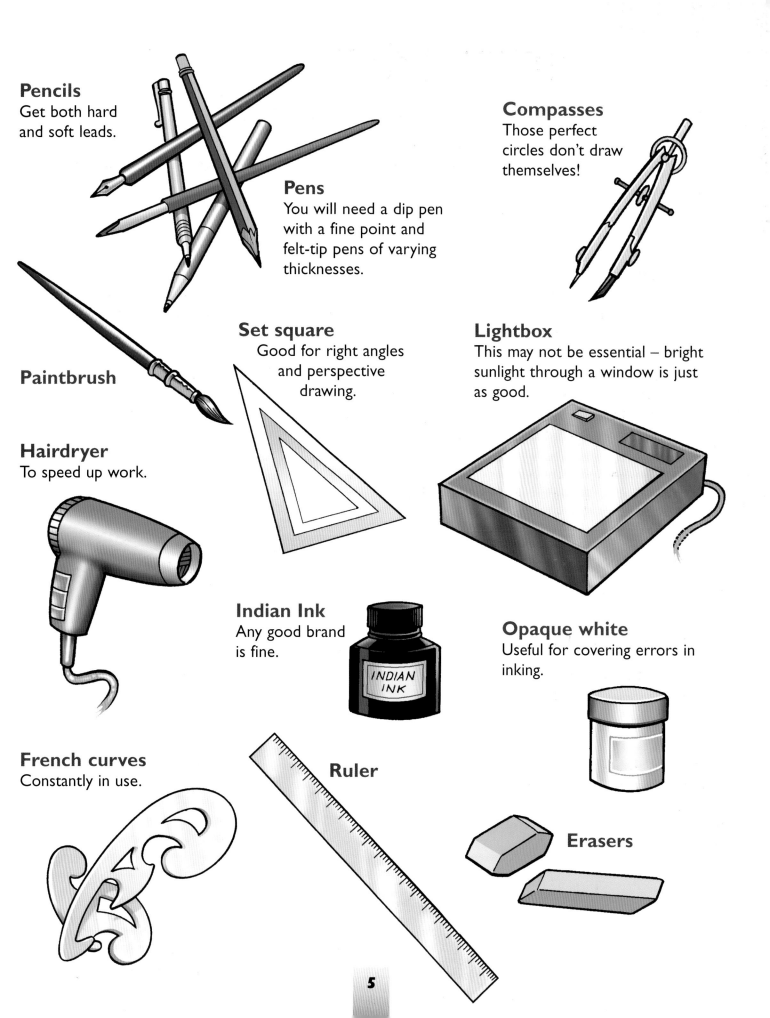

Pencils
Get both hard and soft leads.

Pens
You will need a dip pen with a fine point and felt-tip pens of varying thicknesses.

Compasses
Those perfect circles don't draw themselves!

Paintbrush

Set square
Good for right angles and perspective drawing.

Lightbox
This may not be essential – bright sunlight through a window is just as good.

Hairdryer
To speed up work.

Indian Ink
Any good brand is fine.

INDIAN INK

Opaque white
Useful for covering errors in inking.

French curves
Constantly in use.

Ruler

Erasers

Perspective

When you look at an object, it appears different depending on the angle or distance you view it from. This is called perspective. In all art, from realistic painting to cartoons, an understanding of perspective is absolutely essential.

Basic perspective

If you place cube A so it's facing you straight on (cube B), you'll see that the two side lines look as though they're coming together, or converging (cube C). The point where they meet is the horizon line. This is called one-point perspective.

With cube D, we can follow the converging lines to two meeting points, an example of two-point perspective, The cube is below eye level as it's positioned below the horizon line, allowing us to see the top of it.

The line of sight

The line of sight is the imaginary line that starts from the viewer – the spectator point – and travels into infinity. The place where the line of sight crosses the horizon line of the picture is called the centre point.

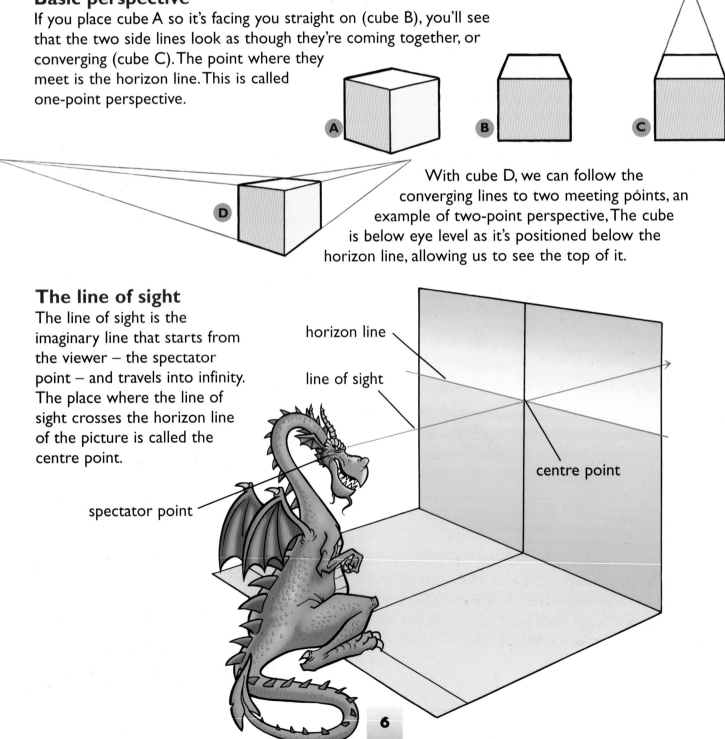

horizon line

line of sight

centre point

spectator point

Vanishing point

Here's an example of one-point perspective. It's the most basic form of perspective, where all the lines retreating from the spectator point converge at a single point, known as the vanishing point.

Worm's-eye view

The worm's-eye view takes the spectator point right down to ground level, or even below, so the viewpoint is at the same level or below the horizon line. This gives the subject a dramatic, imposing feel, as befits a fearsome dragon like this one!

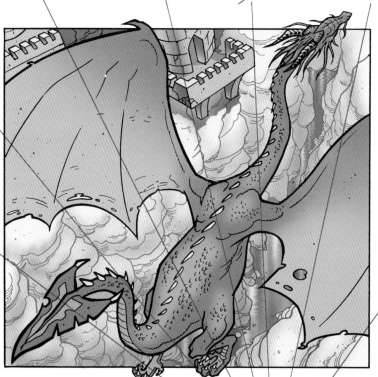

Bird's-eye view

This view sweeps the spectator high above the ground. The higher the horizon line, the higher the viewpoint and, in this example, the horizon line is so high that it's way out of the frame! This gives the spectator an unusual vista – a dragon's-eye view, you might say!

Meet the Dragons

There are many different types of dragon to be found around the world. In this book we shall be meeting three.

Western Dragon

The Western dragon is a cold-hearted reptile that uses its fiery breath to leave burning destruction in its wake. With its scheming eyes, sharp teeth, and tearing claws, it jealously guards its hoard of stolen gold and jewels. Its head and back are covered in armoured scales, horns and spikes, making it all but indestructible. The only known way to kill it is with a lance hurled down its throat.

Eastern Dragon

This Eastern dragon is from Asia, where it is regarded with great affection. It is most frequently found close to the stream, river or lake where its underwater lair is hidden. The female carries her eggs with her for safety and these are sometimes mistaken for pearls. It is said that this dragon protects water carriers and boatmen.

North American Dragon

The North American dragon is famed among native tribes for knowing all the secrets of the world. It is closely associated with nature and the forces that govern the natural order. Unfortunately, due to humankind's plundering of the Earth's resources, this dragon is now rarely seen.

Western Dragon

STAGE 1

Step 1
Start by drawing your 'centre line' – the curve of the dragon's body. Add a circle as a guide to where the dragon's skull will be, plus a smaller one for the tip of his nose.

Step 2
Build a rough stick figure for the arms and legs, with circles for the elbow or knee joints. The arms are fairly human, but the legs definitely belong to a lizard.

Step 3
Roughly plan your wing shape, one slightly folded, the other stretched fully out. The wingspan is roughly equal to the measurement from its nose to its tail.

Step 4
The tip of the tail will feature a sharp, arrow-like point.

STAGE 2

Step 1
Start to build the body, fleshing it out by adding ovals to your stick figure, and sketch in the horns and jaws.

Step 2
Build up the wing supports, which are joined to the dragon's back at the shoulder blades.

Step 3
Add an oval for the triangular tail-tip, plus two long ovals for the feet, which need to be strong enough to bear the dragon's great weight.

Step 4
Define the wings a bit more, adding lines where the 'fingers' that support the large, feathered wings will be.

STAGE 3

Step 1
Carefully start to construct the head and body, adding lines to indicate how you would like the head and body shape to develop.

Step 2
Draw circles where the knuckles and joints on the hands will be. Add in the claws. Do the same for the feet.

Step 3
Shape the triangle at the end of the tail.

Step 4
Do a bit more work on the wings, developing the fingers and the large claws on the top of the wings.

STAGE 4

Step 1
Your dragon should be shaping up nicely now. Add the teeth, and give more shape to the flame blasting from its mouth.

Step 2
Lightly sketch in the line where the front body scales will descend from its throat all the way to the tip of the tail. Note how the tail twists over towards the tip.

Step 3
Carefully build up the hands, giving greater definition to the fingers and claws, and do the same for the feet. Add claws to the ends of its wing fingers.

Step 4
Roughly sketch in the jagged spikes that run down its back from the head to the tip of the tail.

Step 5
Give more shape to the claws on top of its wings.

STAGE 5

Step 1
This is the final pencil stage. Draw in the leathery flaps that hang down from the dragon's jaws, add the scales over its eyes and the shine to its horn ridges.

Step 2
Draw the scales down the front of its body and indicate the overlapping scales over the rest of it.

Step 3
Add a few lines to indicate a worn, leathery feel to its wings.

Step 4
Shape the arrow-tipped tail and add a couple of sharp spikes to the two back points.

STAGE 6

Step 1
Begin by inking in the outline using a fairly bold line. A brush pen is pretty good for this.

Step 2
To achieve the long, smooth line that is needed for the wing supports, use your French curves. A felt-tip and dip pen are best for inking these.

Step 3
Using a much thinner line, ink in the scales on your dragon's body and all the other small details.

Step 4
Again, the French curves come to the rescue when inking in the curve of the tail.

STAGE 7

Step 1
The Western dragon's rough, scaly skin is olive green. Use a paler shade of this colour wherever the light hits it.

Step 2
The dragon's underbelly is shaded in a way to make the skin look taut and muscular over the thick ridges.

Step 3
The horns are a gunmetal colour. Note how these have been shaded to highlight their deep ridges. The claws are a lighter shade of the same colour.

Step 4
The tip of the tail is two-tone, combining the main colour of the dragon's skin and the lighter shade of its underbelly.

Step 5
The inside of the wings is a speckled lime-green colour.

Eastern Dragon

STAGE 1

Step 1
With a smooth sweep of your hand, draw the flowing centre line that will decide the position of your dragon's body.

Step 2
Now add the two circles for the head – a large one for the skull and a smaller one for the snout.

Step 3
Add the arms next, a centre circle for the breastbone and circles for the elbow joints and the hands. These are joined by lines that will become the limbs.

Step 4
Draw the legs next, following the same procedure as for step 3. Draw the centre circle where the hips would be.

Step 4
Now add a large oval for the end of the tail.

STAGE 2

Step 1
Start to build up the head, drawing lines to indicate the jaws, nose, horns, whiskers and flowing hair.

Step 2
To get a sense of the thickness and feel of the dragon's body, draw a series of ovals. Imagine they're solid, which will help when 'fleshing out' in the later stages.

Step 3
Use different shapes and sizes of ovals to build the bulk of the arms. Use triangles for the fingers and toes of this species, as the knuckles aren't as round as those of the Western dragon.

Step 4
The legs are much stronger than the arms, with more bulky muscle, so make the ovals for these rounder.

STAGE 3

Step 1
Start to shape the flowing hair under the jaw and the cheeks, the thick, feathered lashes around the large, oval eyes and the deer-like horns.

Step 2
Build up the arms with sharp, straight lines, going over your ovals and circles. Indicate where the arm feathers will appear.

Step 3
Define the outer body shape and add a guideline for the back ridge. Note how the back ridge is angled in such a way that, at various points, we see both sides of the beast's body.

Step 4
Again, with straighter lines, build up the shape of the legs and add your rough design for the leg feathering.

Step 5
Still using sharp, angular lines, start to shape the tail feather.

STAGE 4

Step 1
The head is almost finished now. Draw the pupils in the eyes. Add the bumps on the top of his skull, and start to detail the hair around the eyes, cheeks and jaw line.

Step 2
Following your back ridge line, draw in the large back spikes. These are widely spaced near the head, but merge into a continual line towards the tip of the tail.

Step 3
Bearing in mind how the dragon's body twists back on itself, mark in the scale lines of the underbelly.

Step 4
Build up the muscle definition in the arms, hands, legs and feet.

Step 5
The tail feathering is taking shape, too. Draw a combination of single and bunched strands.

STAGE 5

Step 1
Add the patterned scales on the head. Draw in the teeth and eyes more clearly.

Step 2
Add scales to the arms and fingers, and detail to the hair on the arms. Note that the scales on the arms get smaller as they descend towards the fingers. They also follow the contours of the muscles. Do the same with the legs.

Step 3
Cover the whole body with squarish scales. Eastern dragons have fish-like scales, in contrast to the armour-like, triangular scales of Western dragons. Finish off the large spikes on the dragon's back.

Step 4
Add a few lines in the centre of the tail feather to give the appearance of a slight sheen.

STAGE 6

Step 1
The whiskers are the trickiest to ink. Trying to keep a steady hand while maintaining a smooth line over a relatively long curve can take quite a bit of practice! Again, French curves certainly help.

Step 2
The main outline of the body is drawn with a thicker line. Try a watercolour brush or a thick, felt-tip pen.

Step 3
The upper-body and underbelly scales should be inked with a fine-nibbed pen. This stage may take a bit of time, but it has to be done.

Step 4
Still with the fine-nibbed pen, ink in the highlights on the claws on both the hands and feet.

Step 5
With careful inking, the arm, leg and tail feathers should look glossy.

STAGE 7

Step 1
The main body of the Asian Eastern dragon is a deep, fiery red-orange with a subtle satin sheen, which ripples along the animal's body as it moves.

Step 2
The lips are light blue, as are the eyelashes, which also have a silky sheen to them.

Step 3
The long, curling whiskers start red, but take on a blue tinge towards the end.

Step 4
The fingers and toes are slightly paler than the rest of the body, and the claws are the same colour as the horns, as they're made of the same substance.

North American Dragon

STAGE 1

Step 1
Have a think about how you would like your dragon to fill the page and then pencil in your centre line.

Step 2
Add a rectangle for the skull and two triangles for the upper and lower jaws.

Step 3
Now pencil in a stick figure, using dots for the joints and straight lines for the limbs.

Step 4
Roughly shape the wings, which are always positioned near the shoulder blades. Place dots where the joints will be and single lines for the wing supports.

STAGE 2

Step 1
Use rectangular blocks to contruct the head and neck, following your centre line.

Step 2
Using the previously drawn dots and lines as guides, add blocks for the arms and legs. Use circles and curved lines for the fingers, toes and claws.

Step 3
Construct the dragon's body with rectangular blocks. The upper body should have a larger block than the lower hip section. A dragon of this size needs a deep chest and large back muscles to carry its weight in flight.

Step 4
The tail of this dragon ends in a hard, leathery flap of skin shaped like a feather. For now, just sketch in the rough shape you would like it to be.

Step 5
Build up the wing arms and supports using little rectangles to indicate the joints. Double up your lines on the wing supports to give them body.

STAGE 3

Step 1
Sketch in the four horns on top of the head, add eyebrow ridges, shape the jaws and add a long, snaking tongue. Finally, add the ears.

Step 2
Shape the arms and legs, as well as the hands, feet and claws, not forgetting the dewclaws at the back of each leg.

Step 3
Shape the body and the sweeping curve of the tail.

Step 4
At the top of each wing, sketch in a large claw. Most dragons with leathery wings have these. They're sometimes used as extra weapons, though with sharp talons and teeth, not to mention fiery breath, they're rarely needed!

Step 5
Draw in the large, triangular spikes that run down the spine. On North American dragons they don't continue all the way down to the tail.

STAGE 4

Step 1
Start to build up the contours of the head. Add the teeth, nostrils and cheek spikes.

Step 2
Shape the muscles in the shoulders, arms and hands. Then do the same with the hips, legs and feet.

Step 3
Develop the leathery tail feather more clearly by adding holes and wear and tear to the edges.

Step 4
Smooth out the hard edges of the wing joints and wing claws, then add lines to indicate wrinkled skin where the visible wing joins the dragon's back.

Step 5
Round off the sharp edges to the back spikes, giving them all a backward slant.

STAGE 5

Step 1
Draw in the scales over the eyes and around the mouth. Add two thin, flowing chin whiskers, wrinkles under the eyes and the sharp little facial scales on the head.

Step 2
Darken up the pencil lines on the underbelly scales and sketch in the scales over the hands and feet. Darken all your pencil lines for clarity.

Step 3
Sketch in the bumps on the wing supports and the little claws on the wing tips – a few holes and tears in the wing membranes will give them a battle-worn look.

Step 4
Now sketch in the overlapping, squarish body scales, bearing in mind the contours of the dragon's body.

Step 5
When you draw the scales on the tail, remember that the size and angle of the scales should gradually alter as the tail curves away from the viewer.

STAGE 6

Step 1
Carefully ink over the final pencil lines of the dragon's outline, starting with the head. A brush pen is ideal for this.

Step 2
Once the outline is inked, use a fine line to ink in the smaller details, such as the scales on the head, hands and feet.

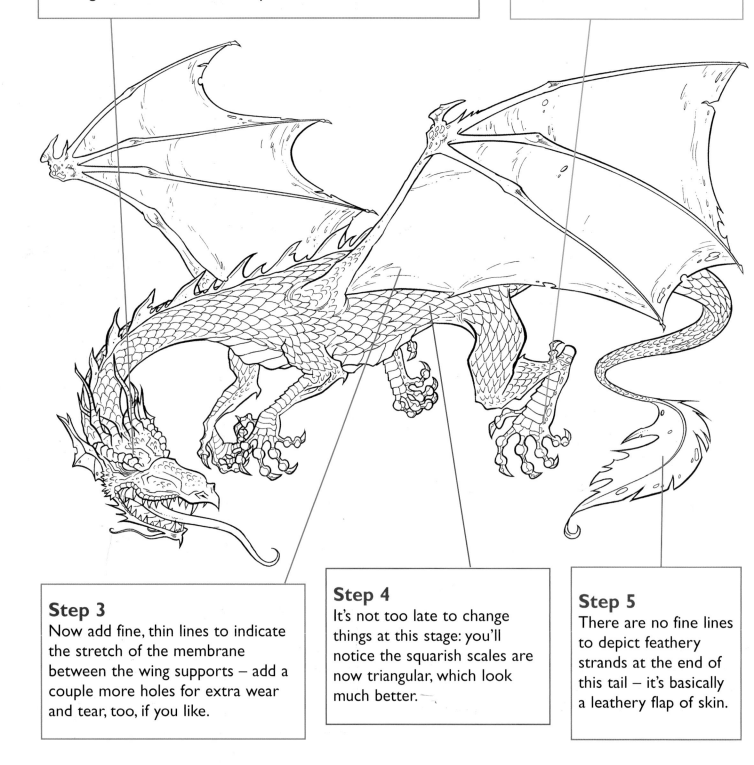

Step 3
Now add fine, thin lines to indicate the stretch of the membrane between the wing supports – add a couple more holes for extra wear and tear, too, if you like.

Step 4
It's not too late to change things at this stage: you'll notice the squarish scales are now triangular, which look much better.

Step 5
There are no fine lines to depict feathery strands at the end of this tail – it's basically a leathery flap of skin.

STAGE 7

Step 1
The wings of this large dragon are a slightly deeper blue than the rest of its body.

Step 2
The scales on the dragon's body are a metallic blue to emphasize their hard, shiny quality. Warriors who manage to slay these beasts have been known to prise off their back scales, rivetting them together to make fine body armour.

Step 3
The horns are extremely strong and coloured a deep, shiny blue-black. The eyes shimmer with a fiery glow.

Step 4
The scales on the underbelly are not as strong as the smaller back scales and, if struck at the right angle, can be pierced by a sharp arrow or spear.

Step 5
The tip of the tail is made from the same leathery substance as the wings, but the edges are very sharp and can inflict deep cuts to unprotected skin.

Glossary

angular Having angles or sharp corners.

centre line The starting point of any stick figure, indicating the position of the figure's body.

compass A device involving a needle and a pencil hinged together at one end, used for drawing circles.

contour The outline or shape of something.

converge Come together.

dewclaw A short, functionless claw on the foot of certain animals.

French curve A piece of plastic with curved edges and curved shapes cut out of it to help illustrators draw curves.

glossy Having a smooth, shiny surface.

hoard A store of something such as money or treasure.

horizon line The line where land or sea appears to meet the sky. In perspective drawing it is the line along which converging lines, extended from the sides of an object, meet.

infinity Limitless time, space or distance.

inflict Cause (usually damage or harm).

joint Any of the parts of the body where bones are connected.

lair A place where a wild animal, such as a dragon, rests or sleeps.

lance A long weapon with a metal point.

light box A flat box with a light inside it that shines through the box's transparent plastic top. A light box can be used to illuminate a drawing so that its lines can be retraced on another sheet of paper placed above it.

membrane A thin, flexible sheet of skin or tissue.

opaque Not transparent.

perspective In drawing, changing the relative size and appearance of objects to allow for the effects of distance.

plunder *verb* Steal, causing damage in the process.

procession A group of people moving forward in a line as part of a celebration.

rivet *verb* Fasten using short metal rods (called rivets) that are passed through holes in materials and then flattened at both ends.

satin *adjective* Smooth and glossy like satin, a fabric made from silk or rayon.

set square A flat instrument in the shape of a triangle, used to draw lines at particular angles.

sheen A bright, softly shining surface.

shoulder blades The large, flat triangular bones at the top of the back that join with the upper arm bones.

spectator point The point from which a picture is viewed.

stick figure A simple drawing of a person or creature with single lines for the torso, arms and legs.

vanishing point In perspective drawing, the point on the horizon line where two converging lines, extended from the sides of an object, meet.

vista A scenic view.

watercolour Paint made by mixing pigments (substances that give something its colour) with water.

Further Information

Books

Creating Creatures of Fantasy and Imagination: Everyday Inspiration for Painting Fairies, Elves, Dragons and More by Claudia Nice (North Light Books, 2005)

DragonArt: How to Draw Fantastic Dragons and Fantasy Creatures by Jessica Peffer (Impact Books, 2005)

Drawing and Painting Fantasy Beasts by Kev Walker (David and Charles, 2005)

Drawing and Painting Fantasy Figures: From the Imagination to the Page by Finlay Cowan (David and Charles, 2004)

How to Draw Wizards, Dragons and other Magical Creatures by Barbara Soloff Levy (Dover Publications, 2004)

Websites

drawsketch.about.com/od/drawingdragons/
Advice on drawing dragons.

elfwood.lysator.liu.se/farp/art.html
A guide to creating your own fantasy art, including dragons.

neondragonart.com/dp/
Another online dragon-drawing tutorial.

www.dreslough.com/main/tutorials.htm
Yet more guidance on dragons and how to draw them.

Note to parents and teachers:

Every effort has been made by the publishers to ensure that these websites are suitable for children and contain no inappropriate or offensive material. However, because of the nature of the Internet, it is impossible to guarantee that the contents of these sites will not be altered. We strongly advise that Internet access is supervised by a responsible adult.

Index